Navigations: Scoring the Moment

Contents

01	Taking a Bearing	5
02	Plotting	19
03	Adventures	39
04	Correspondences	53

Acknowledgements	60
Contributors	62

TAKING A BEARING

01

to relocate	to reposition
to move	to orientate

In 2018, I answered an email from John Bingham-Hall (Director of Theatrum Mundi) and Ellie Cosgrave (then Director of UCL Urban Innovation and Policy Lab and Associate Professor in Urban Innovation and Policy at University College London) inviting me to participate in a short research event they were planning. This activity was part of the larger research project John and Ellie were conducting at the time, which eventually led to the publication of their seminal paper *Choreographing the city: Can dance practice inform the engineering of sustainable urban environments?*[1] They invited me to partner with an engineer and jointly observe and reflect on a particular city junction (Great Portland Street, London). John and Ellie wished to compare how a choreographer (myself) and an engineer (Aaron Matthew) would see the same city intersection from the different perspectives of our disciplines.

Then, in 2019, another invitation from John Bingham-Hall arrived in my inbox. This time I was offered a fellowship at Theatrum Mundi, spurred by an interest in furthering ideas discussed in John and Ellie's paper, with a particular interest in how the city shapes our bodies and how, in turn, we shape the city. By 'shape', I mean the actual physical experiences of movement in and around buildings through which muscles and spatial awareness develop. This development is borne out of the unique experiences of the specific city one is a part of. There are cities that are *walking cities* or *driving cities*; there are quiet, loud, fast, slow, broad or high cities, and the bodies within them are shaped by the need to navigate them. A city's attributes shape our postures and reflexes; in other words, they shape how our

bodies move. Urban designers, engineers, architects, exhibition curators and choreographers share a common interest in how we create movement around, in, and through a site; how we direct bodies in what they see, what they hear, and when they stop or start to travel; how we manage the flow of people and things to form an identifiable *Place*. In turn, the physicality of sensations (shape, texture, size, speed) of a site influences how we identify ourselves within that Place. This identification becomes formalised into seeing ourselves as part of specific communities and contributes to the development of a sense of our *position* in society more broadly. As the fellowship commenced, I began a number of long-lasting conversations with urban designers, engineers, architects and exhibition curators.

---

1   Bingham-Hall, J. and E. Cosgrave (2019)
    'Choreographing the city: Can dance practice inform
    the engineering of sustainable urban environments?'
    Mobilities, 14(2), 188–203.

Dear Adesola,

Our lovely conversation of many months ago, and the memories it evoked, continues to echo in my mind. We spoke about being present, about connection, about the impact of a place, its physical and symbolic characteristics, about the tempo that is created through a collection of bodies, about being free in the body, or not, about the moment and how this relates to exhibitions. Our conversation transported me back to a moment six years ago when we opened an exhibition at the Royal Academy of Arts featuring an installation by Grafton Architects titled *Sensing Spaces: Architecture Reimagined* (2014), which aspired to bring the visceral experience of architecture to the fore and heighten the awareness of everyday spatial encounters. Light reflected off a structure in Grafton's installation, sequenced to emulate the natural changes in tone and intensity throughout the day and seasons.

I saw a child move out of the shadows into the light as it shifted slowly acros the floor. They spun with their arms outstretched, looking upward. There was no sound in the installation, just the light in which they played, danced, moved. At one point, they dropped to the ground, rolled and got up again. Other children joined them, making their own movements. I stood in the shadows and observed. Some adults were otherwise absorbed and oblivious to the children's play, while others around me noticed too. Despite the relative darkness, I could make out smiles on their faces.

One audience member's – the child's – response to the installation was performed for other members of the audience to witness. We were all involved in this action, empathetically connected to the child, to those around, to the space and time. Memories were triggered of unconscious bodily expressions: to delight and to be delighted. Equally, questions arose about the positive and negative reactions architecture can inspire, influencing behaviour and social dynamics. The Royal Academy, by its name, reputation, building and location, conveys an established authority and, associated with this, an air of elitism. This child was unaware of that context, or at least undaunted by it, and was free to play and express what the installation inspired within them. The child's response gave the installation another layer of meaning, where the cyclic oscillation of light was intertwined with expressive movement.

As you and I talked about moving through a city, I saw parallels with exhibitions and their potential to be viewed critically through a performative, physiological and bodily lens. Exhibitions provide a physical encounter with a work of art or an object in a constructed world removed from the distractions of everyday life. The audience is wanting and willing to be stimulated intellectually and emotionally and is thus attuned to the surroundings and seeking encounters. A visit to an exhibition is a social activity, happening in the company of others, known or unknown, and generating both an individual and collective experience. An exhibition in an institution has the additional dimension of carrying that institution's reputation and stigma and, in the case of paid exhibitions, that of a transactional exchange that impacts audiences' psychology.

To varying degrees, works and ideas are staged, positioned to form a narrative, overt or implied, and the audience needs to find an individual and collective rhythm in response to them and their installation. The mesmerising power of a work can be amplified by collective viewing, with the sensation of awe felt throughout a room. Māori artist Lisa Reihana's immersive thirty-two-minute panoramic video installation *in Pursuit of Venus [infected]*, on show during the *Oceania* exhibition (2018), had such an effect. This video, as a provocative moving-image interpretation of the French scenic wallpaper *Les Sauvages de la Mer Pacifique*, challenges stereotypes and returns the imperial gaze. The durational work slowed the pace of the visitor thereafter. Rhythmic changes to the visitor's behaviour were also utilised as a critical tool in *Sensing Spaces*, triggered by sensory shifts such as the light and shadow in Grafton's installation or entering a dark space with a delicate bamboo structure infused with the scent of tatami by Japanese architect Kengo Kuma.

We exist in a state of flow with our surroundings – a rich, ongoing dialogue – that we are often barely cognisant of. In *Sensing Spaces*, spatial propositions were made to critique and challenge the behavioural dialogue. Frances Kéré, an architect born in Burkina Faso who moved to Germany in his late teens, created a tunnel squeezing visitors into closer proximity than he had observed the European audience would be comfortable with. This echoed Edward T. Hall's studies of proxemics (human spatial behaviours), published in his book *The Hidden Dimension* in 1966, that showed different proxemic relations across cultures. The installation also invited visitors to place coloured straws into the perforated structure of the tunnel, triggering interaction and unexpected creative responses. This installation instigated a noticeable change in how people carried themselves through the rest of the show: bodies were more relaxed, moving at closer distances from each other, and being more engaged with one another, as judged by a rise in the auditory atmosphere in the galleries.

As a curator and creator, I am excited by how the conceptual and intellectual ideas of an exhibition can be enhanced or foregrounded by utilising performative thinking in their creation and considering the audience's bodies in space. Furthermore, the score of exhibitions can be controlled and orchestrated akin to, but more easily than, spaces within a city, which offers the possibility of using the staging of exhibitions as testing grounds for real-world, spatial, social, political and embodied situations. There are many more conversations to explore on the topic.

With fond wishes and curiosity,
Kate Goodwin
Head/Curator of Architecture, Royal Academy of Arts
London, March 2021

During the first part of my fellowship in 2019, which I titled Choreographing the City: at/as the city limits, I was particularly interested in exploring how a city shapes different bodies differently: the experience of female bodies, non-binary bodies, homeless bodies, Black bodies, for instance. Depending on how one's physical body fits with the design, it seems that within the same *site* multiple experiences of *Place* exist. The composed speed, sound and texture of a given city is directed at the physicality of a particular mainstream body (often white, around six-foot, *able*-bodied, employed, heteronormative, and male). While, for those bodies that do not fit these characteristics, the city is experienced, in part, as a process of having to reconfigure their sense of identity in order to avoid being constantly in opposition to the city's design. This reconfiguration is an added layer of being 'shaped' by the city and an added layer of 'shaping' the city (as the city reconfigures itself around *difference* to continue to service the mainstream body).

A classic example of this is a park bench on which a homeless body sleeps. This changes the flow of mainstream – non-homeless – bodies walking through the park, avoiding the bench, unable to sit on it. The bench also shapes the homeless body as the muscles and bones of the sleeping person extend themselves into the long ledge of the bench. The city responds by changing the shape of the bench, adding armrests to create individual sitting areas along the bench. The homeless body is then unable to unfold to sleep. The homeless body reconfigures their shape to sleep sitting upright or reconfigures their location to sleep elsewhere. This is an exchange in which both city and body have reshaped themselves.

In the first phase of the fellowship, I explored the choreography of the city through looking at concepts of *chasing* *stillness*, *lingering in dwelling*, and *residing in wandering*.[2] As part of that process, I danced with people from across a range of disciplines who shared similar interests in Place-making with me. I exchanged ideas with performers, architects, musicians, engineers, and curators, all concerned with how places could be composed/designed/choreographed with equity. We shared a hope that a city shaped by a concern for equity would liberate the experience of beings within it, reaching beyond the bodies of humans to the multiple human and non-human elements of the dance of the city. Findings and reflections from this first phase of my fellowship can be found in *Dance, Architecture and Engineering (Dance in Dialogue)*, a monograph published by Bloomsbury Publishing in 2021.

As my fellowship progressed into a second phase, which I titled Choreographing the City: Navigations, I became drawn to the idea of how the design of the city can become a form of physical logic that generates everyday meaning through bodily experience. I began to question how the activity of moving around the city composes everyday meaning-making to generate city as an ethical practice. After all, coming from the embodied sensitivities of a dance background, I see the body as the vessel through which perceptions are registered. The brain, mind, spirit and body come together as awareness and consciousness, sensing the poetics of responding to the surrounding world.

When I write about the body here, I am assuming a mind-full-spirited-body. Many practices involved in health and well-being point out that when we change our bodies, we change our brain's processes: we

---

2   See my monograph: Akinleye, A. (2021) *Dance, Architecture, and Engineering.*

change our mind's meaning-making. For instance, Phil Parker's Lightning Process or Eric Franklin's Franklin Method, through their scientific research, conclude that the physicality of the body changes the physicality of the brain and changes one's 'mind' about the experience of everyday activities. Similarly, psychiatrist, author, and researcher Bessel van der Kolk, in works such as *The Body Keeps the Score*,[3] describes how the experiencing, sensing body shapes the brain, and the brain's response to the sensual register of the body, in turn, shapes the reality of consciousness. From my humanities – dance – perspective, and influenced by Africanist and Indigenous scholars and worldviews, I too feel that the body, brain, mind and environment are all part of the same network, continually creating each other. To describe this co-created, emergent reality, feminist theorist and philosopher Karen Barad suggests the term *intra-action*:

> *'Intra-action' signifies the mutual constitution of entangled agencies. That is, in contrast to the usual 'interaction', which assumes that there are separate individual agencies that precede their interaction, the notion of intra-action recognizes that distinct agencies do not precede, but rather emerge through, their intra-action.*[4]

So, when I suggest that the body changes shape to respond to the city, I assume the brain changes, and with it, one's meaning-making and responses change too; everything is in change together: city, brain, mind, body, and thus reality. The experience of the shape of my body lying down on the park bench includes emotions and thoughts that are changed by the sensation of trying to sleep sitting upright or over the armrests that divide the bench. Importantly, this crafts a form of meaning for the sum of myself and park bench. Thus, through movement, we shape the meaning of the city, and the city shapes the meaning of us.

Through continued collaborations with colleagues in architecture, engineering, curation, music, and dance, I started to feel confident that we were not just discovering how movement responds to the aesthetic design of the city but were also exploring the meaning-making and responsibility that movement within the city generates. Within the discussion, discovery, and interrogation of meaning-making across our transdisciplinary work, there was also a shared spatial ontology (worldview). I became interested in how we could make this ontology more explicit despite the vernacular of our different practices. I wondered if there was the prospect of a shared *language* that could emerge from our verbal and movement discussions.

The transdisciplinary context we were working in also had the potential to reveal a lexicon that encompassed the thought-based and physical-based processes of meaning-making we were engaging with. My hope was to identify a lexicon that could offer modes to liberate our communication from the contingencies and limitations of our different 'subject' areas. I wondered if the shared set of words of a lexicon could sharpen the tools for tracking our individual and collective meaning-making.

3   For more on this, see Van der Kolk, B. (2014) *The Body Keeps the Score: Brain, Mind, and Body in the Healing of Trauma.*

4   Barad, K. (2007) *Meeting the Universe Halfway: Quantum Physics and the Entanglement of Matter and Meaning*, p. 33.

Starting Point

Amid the interdisciplinary collaborations that were central to my fellowship, I offered contemporary dance as a non-verbal language that could be co-created during movement workshops. As we worked together, I noticed that the somatic – non-verbal – language of dance had sometimes become a temporary *universal* language for bringing the *bodily* of experience to the fore. But it was important to acknowledge that dance is not a singular practice. There are many dance forms, and thus it could be argued there are many bodily languages to be offered. Nor could dance provide neutral language. Within dance, just as within verbal languages, there are disciplinary customs of meaning and classicisms.

I was situated in a dance form (Western contemporary dance) that brings its own paradigms, but paradoxically, my attraction to collaborative projects necessitated an exploration beyond the classicisms of my own dance world. Collaborating with colleagues who shared the same interest in spatial practices but came from different fields required me to engage in a process of my own *disorienting relocation*, which included challenging myself to find new dance-making processes within my own practice. I noticed how familiar, well-worn Western dance canons acted like beacons of recognition for me. But the brightness of these beacons was what I wanted to avoid rather than be drawn towards, mothlike. My aim was to find my bearings without regressing to the familiar doctrines of my dance training. This was a shared objective amongst collaborators. We all attempted to avoid the habitual routes of our initial Western training, thinking/feeling/moving beyond the binary structures commonly present within our respective disciplines that can also be traps, perpetuating colonialism and misogyny.

Working collaboratively gave me new perspectives that illuminated my desire to develop processes for navigating away from the familiarity of my own disciplinary starting coordinates. Fortunately, transdisciplinary ways of working always introduce me to concepts outside my own dance practice that, once understood, irreversibly change the way I consider a topic, raising questions that I have previously been unaware of. Educationalists Ray Land and J. H. F. Meyer call the ideas that offer irreversible illumination of thought *threshold concepts*.[5] I feel that the experiences of paradigm shifts were also what attracted other collaborators to our shared project. We were all interested in how the habitually unarticulated within a given discipline can be exposed by someone from outside the field. Without this exposure, perceptions and meaning can remain assumed, lost in disciplinary rhetoric and custom, lost to being questioned from within. At the same time, these assumptions can offer stimulating questions for those from outside the given discipline.

Being introduced to the threshold concepts of my collaborators during the fellowship led me to question the impact my dance practice has on how I mentally and physically police my own ability to discover something new. For instance, familiarity with modes of communication within my own field of dance can lead to me assuming meanings beyond the words or movements I use to express something. These assumptions in language can cloud

5   Land, R., J. H. F Meyer, and J. Smith (eds.)(2008) *Threshold Concepts within the Disciplines*; Meyer, J. and R. Land (2003) 'Threshold Concepts and Troublesome Knowledge: Linkages to Ways of Thinking and Practising within the Disciplines'. *ETL project* [https://www.etl.tla.ed.ac.uk/docs/ETLreport4.pdf].

communication and become more visible when working in a transdisciplinary way. However, they also often manifest a useful vagueness that is rendered by grasping at the change in perspective offered by a colleague in a different discipline. I feel that these slippages of meaning signpost the most intriguing areas for excavation. The 'failure' in communication, caused by unfamiliarity/familiarity with the use of language and movement, is so valuable in transdisciplinary collaborations. Given these perceptual shifts caused by our (unpredictable) communication across the disciplines of people who share interests in spatial practices and Place-making, I noticed that there were some repeated words and ideas that seemed to resonate with all of us. These ideas and words became the starting point for a shared spatial practices lexicon.

During the latter part of my fellowship at Theatrum Mundi and at my subsequent residency at the Massachusetts Institute of Technology (MIT), I explored this spatial practice lexicon. I hoped that the exploration of the lexicon would nourish transdisciplinary communication. Following philosopher and educational reformer John Dewey's discussion in *Experience and Nature*, first published in 1925, I assumed that the communication itself causes the ideas.[6] This suggests that the language of our communication is rarely as all-encompassing as the idea itself. Our ideas are much bigger than the *equipment* we use for communication. Ideas have to shape themselves into whatever communicable instruments are available, and in doing so, some of the inner narrative of the idea is lost to the language. For this reason, when I propose an emerging lexicon in this publication, I refer to the components of the lexicon as *worded-ideas* to suggest

that I engage across the spectrum of mind (thoughts – words), body (somatics – actions) and environment (ecosystems – emergences). The lexicon I propose is interchangeably a lexicon of words and/or a lexicon of actions and/or a lexicon of emergences.

The ten worded-ideas, which I introduce below, resonated in and were repeated across many of the conversations I had within the multiple disciplines of Place-making. Despite slight differences in meaning, these worded-ideas revealed shared epistemologies and ontological perspectives, shared beyond the limits of the linguistics of our communications. In workshops and talks with others during my fellowship, these worded-ideas seemed to cut across the syntax of our communication, as well as the syntax of the buildings we moved around (or sat in, using our computers), and the syntax of dance styles we were working with. While crafting the lexicon, I questioned if the process itself would provide new opportunities to communicate experience through the wider context of transdisciplinary togetherness.

The worded-ideas of the lexicon:

- CONNECTEDNESS/SEPARATEDNESS[7]
- (AT LEAST) FOUR-DIMENSIONAL DISTANCE
- AGENCY
- GROWTH
- POWER
- RESISTANCE
- BOUNDARY
- PRECISENESS
- IMPROVISATION
- SCORE

7   'Separatedness' is an invented word that aims to describe the quality of splitting, dividing (separated: separatedness) but not a quality of being distinct, isolated, or detached (separate: separateness, which is an existent word).

6   Dewey, J. (1958) *Experience and Nature*.

In the following chapters, I have loosely drawn inspiration from the activity of urban orienteering as an allegorical structure for exploring the worded-ideas. Orienteering, a sport that requires navigational skills using a map, is described by British Orienteering as 'exciting and challenging exercises of navigation using mind and body'.[8] Coming from the position of emplacement through dance, I see the activities of dancing, reflecting, and researching as similar to the exercises of mind-full-body in environment (following Dewey's matrix of mind-body-environment).[9]

In the following chapter, PLOTTING, I plot the worded-ideas as components of an urban orienteering map to capture what emerged through numerous and multifaceted exchanges (spoken, drawn, sung, written, danced) with collaborators. This chapter is not so much an effort to define the worded-ideas but more a space in which to introduce some of the attributes that can locate them within the lexicon and in relation to all the other worded-ideas. I wander around the worded-ideas by sharing some of the dancing and thinking that came up while I was exploring their meaning.

In the next chapter, ADVENTURES, I share my practice of *moment-ist dance-walks*: a method I developed for the exploration of the worded-ideas through the physicality of walks around my local city streets during Covid-19 lockdowns and while recovering from long Covid. They reveal how the relationships between the worded-ideas can construct a new experiential city-body.

In the final chapter, CORRESPONDANCES, I outline what emerged from the exploration of the worded-ideas as coordinates in the city and offer some conclusions from my navigations of the meaning-making of the city. This chapter looks at ideas of moments (a moment being awareness of the elements of the situation that forms the assemblage of now) and responsiveness (responsiveness being the action or meaning-making stimulated by the situation that forms the assemblage of now).

8   See more about orienteering on the British Orienteering website: https://www. britishorienteering.org.uk.

9   See Boydston, J. A. (ed.)(2008) *The Later Works of John Dewey, 1925–1953 (Vol. 4: The Quest for Certainty)*.

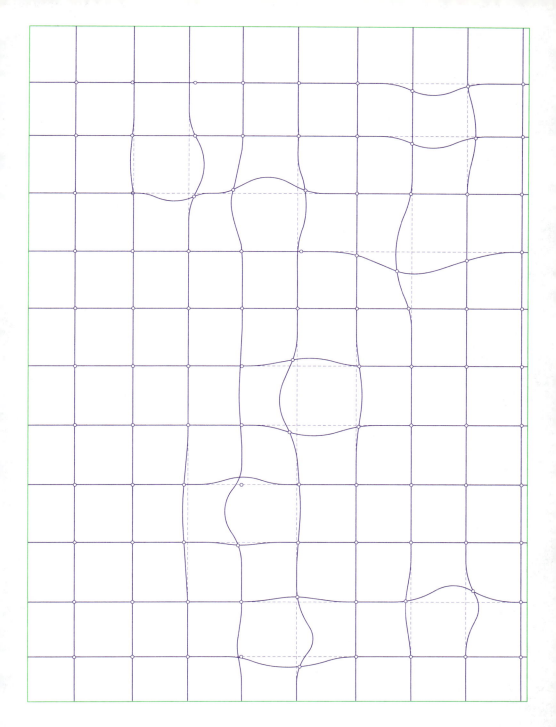

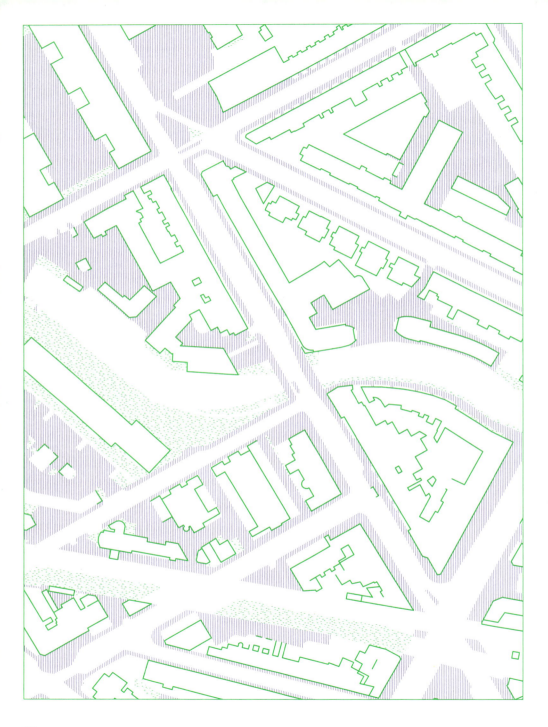

PLOTTING

02

to chart	to map
to formulate	to re-mark

Due to Covid-19, the year 2020 brought a number of lockdowns, making it very difficult to go to a dance studio to conduct research. Collaborative activity moved to interaction via computer screen, particularly the Zoom online platform. The previous year, during the first part of my fellowship, I had been collaborating through visiting architectural practices and holding workshops in and around London. Suddenly, I had to adjust to conversations on Zoom, but wonderfully, this meant that I could collaborate with people in cities all around the world. In October, I hosted a programme with Helen Kindred and Dancing Strong Movement Lab, performing live online as part of a series of Theatrum Mundi's Virtual Roundtables, instigated by John Bingham-Hall, Rennie Tang and Dimitri Szuter. I also co-hosted the *Morning Conversation* podcast series with artist and scholar Gediminas Urbonas, as part of the Art, Culture, and Technology (ACT) programme at MIT, featuring invited artists and scholars.[10]

During these digital gatherings, the idea of being situated meant frantic calculations of time zones and following the updates on regional Covid-19 case numbers. What it was to be present in cities, present in our bodies, was rearticulated by the digital landscape of meetings facilitated by computers. This led me to create new choreographic works titled after the fellowship: Navigations. Navigations used the Zoom algorithm to interrogate the dancing body, which was situated in the city through the Zoom background.

Light disturbs the Zoom background's response to what is human: the subject placed in the foreground in front of the screen. Using light direction, movement and an image of the city in the Zoom background, the algorithm can be induced to accidentally reshape the body of the dancer with the image of the city, and the image of the city can be reshaped by the movement of the dancer. The set of choreographies I made during this time were hybrid live-digital events where each dancer was dancing live within their domestic space and facing a computer screen, which fed back a combination of their dancing body, their domestic space and the city image background. Using the direction of light on the dancer's body, the home space and the city image were interwoven, revealing and reshaping in response to how the dancer moved in relationship to their light source and how the algorithm interpreted what part of the image was the human and what was the background. This movement in dancers' home spaces was broadcast live to a digital audience who joined the Zoom session. Each of the choreographic pieces for the Zoom platform was an intense exploration of a single point in the city through moving within the limits of a photograph used as the Zoom background.

10 For more on this, see the series of eight podcasts produced with ACT, MIT. Akinleye, A. and G. Urbonas (2021) *Choreographing the City*. [Podcast]. Available at: https://player.fm/series/3311938.

Dear Adesola,

This is a letter from a moment during Navigations, a live-digital performance presented via Zoom in June 2020. I have been reflecting on the bodily-spatial encounters of my journey through Navigations' choreographic rehearsals on Zoom: the experiences of navigating relationships between my physical presence, felt sensorial experience, and my projected virtual city environment. While rehearsing within the context of digital performance work, new questions are highlighted for me: what is it to be present, visible, constructive of my environment? I embody these questions, considering the relationships between the bodily, the somatic and the principles of internal sensations and external expressivity, as I move within the city space that is a virtual background projected in my home. I move in relationship with the images of the city that flood the domestic space of my locked-down home.

I enjoy the sensations of almost touching as I seek to investigate the architecture of the projected building, a virtual background landscape imposed upon my corporeal presence through the Zoom screen. The blurring of edges between my skin and the city in this Zoom moment provokes flickering sensations of moving concrete with my moving bones. There are moments of complete invisibility as my body merges into the fabric of the projected building, streets and spaces between them. I soften my limbs into my domestic space, disappearing into the projection of an alleyway, marking the spaces, marking the between-ness of the buildings. I tentatively dip my toes into the edges of the space around me. I lengthen my arms, reaching out to touch, to connect, to feel and taste the space I move into at my distal edges.

Exploring movement in relationship with the virtual environment through improvisation, I question the inner connectivity of my body through a sensorial awareness of the outer expressivity of my moving body in space. The experience of moving within this virtual environment raises questions about the relationship between our lived experiences and the environments we navigate.

Later, as we share the investigative process of Navigations in a live Zoom performance, my perception of presence within my environment alters dramatically. The technology of the virtual background projection relies on light, and the performance is much later the day than the rehearsals. I have very limited light in my home space. This means that, effectively, there is no light to pick up the virtual image in the space. With no virtual background, no alleyway, the projected buildings washed away by the lack of light, and no sense of belonging to the city, I begin to move. Exposed in the reality of my domestic space, I seek the image of the city to move in relationship with. As the performance continues, other performers (with the correct amount of light) successfully navigate their city spaces and home spaces. I am increasingly aware of my lack of access to this space, denied access in this moment to anything other than my domestic space. The presence of my movement in this experience, held only by its internal sensations, is absent of any potential for the outer expressivity of my body. Muted. My actions have no effect. I am unable to penetrate the virtual environment. I feel only the exhaustion of not belonging. No access to the things, the sites, the possibilities for response that others have – it makes me feel lost in a reality that is at odds with that of others. I try to remember the feeling of being held by a place, of touching, of reaching out, navigating. This takes all my energy. All my resources are absent in the moment of being absent.

With love and gratitude,
Helen (Kindred)
February 2021

In the latter part of 2020, in London, the government regulations for the Covid-19 lockdown eased and allowed us to go outside and travel for work, but I still had no access to a dance studio. I started to plot the worded-ideas of the lexicon onto my local London streets, as if they were my dance studio. I investigated a part of a street through the same exploratory movements I had been using when dancing with a photograph of a city street in Zoom. Thus, this chapter shares my exploration of the worded-ideas in the London streets through dancing. I look to the lexicon as a way of drawing out the inner assumptions and habitual meaning-making any one of us has generated from the cities we are familiar with. I hope that by sharing them here, I produce mutual significances within you, the reader. I would like to encourage you to explore the lexicon within the streets of your city or neighbourhood and perhaps adapt or expand the understanding of the worded-ideas to your practice and space. Please stay safe doing so! In 2022, during the second part of my residency at MIT, I shared this very invitation with people visiting the MIT campus as part of the *Choreographing the Campus* programme. The visitors explored the lexicon's worded-ideas through engaging with the architecture of the campus.[11] You might use the lexicon within a specific place to build a sense of knowing or belonging to that place.

The worded-ideas plot an area for exploration. I see them as points of location in collaborative discussions and dances. As with plotting coordinates on an urban orienteering map, I hope that the worded-ideas, the lexicon, indicate pathways of exploration in spatial practices. The worded-ideas are conceived of as relational, and together they create a network rather than existing as separate elements on a list. They create a relational infrastructure for being in a moment of exploring meaning-making on the streets of the city. I have assigned each worded-idea an element from an urban orienteering map, such as walls or roads, giving each worded-idea an allegorical representation in the city. Adopting the orienteering map as a method to get to know the worded-ideas has allowed me to experiment with them as physical elements of the city. For instance, I explore PRECISENESS through dancing on walls or BOUNDARY through dancing by a stream of traffic.

---

11 For more information on *Choreographing the Campus*, see 'Choreographing the Campus with Adesola Akinleye', ACT at MIT. Available at: https://arts.mit.edu/choreographing-the-campus/.

The Exploration of the Lexicon:

I   CONNECTEDNESS/SEPARATEDNESS
II   (AT LEAST) FOUR-DIMENSIONAL DISTANCE
III   AGENCY
IV   GROWTH
V   POWER
VI   RESISTANCE
VII   BOUNDARY
VIII PRECISENESS
IX   IMPROVISATION
X   SCORE

I. CONNECTEDNESS/SEPARATEDNESS

This first worded-idea, CONNECTEDNESS/SEPARATEDNESS, belongs to the part of the lexicon that addresses a reality (or ontology) within which the rest of the worded-ideas are given context and made recognisable.

As I start to perform a dance on the pavement by a traffic light, raising an arm, arching my back, I am responding to the gravity, air, concrete, sound, music, people, breath, trajectory in and around me. The dance of this Place lives in and around me when I lower my arm, twist my back, extend my ribs into the music of the traffic. The dance is what I am doing, what I am entering, what I am feeling, and what I am being. Dance is a visceral illustration of the patterns of connection and separation encountered when moving with the multi-layered, multi-species, multi-dimensional *now-ness* of being in this city. As a choreographer, I envisage the dance of a city (or town, forest, or room) as a way to experience the totality (*us-ness*) of a Place. I also experience a sense of being present with all around me when I am dancing. I flow in and out of being connected to the music of the traffic, hitting a note, twisting away from the sound, breathing in the air that I move through: car exhaust becomes part of me as I hang in suspension on one leg, and then leaves me as I breathe out and sink into a knee bend. Dancing, I am in constant relationship with the world around me in order to be aware of the nuances of the sensation of being present and responding to the moment.

I define CONNECTEDNESS/SEPARATEDNESS as a movement within what Karen Barad calls *intra-action*[12] and Grandma Chipps and Lakota Elders refer to in *Mitákuye*

Oyás'iŋ, the Lakota language confirmation and prayer, which means 'all my relatives' or 'we are all related'.[13] Tongan social anthropologist Hūfanga 'Ōkusitino Māhina (and other Tongan Elders) explain this as the impossibility of stepping out of the sum of everything (as defined in the tā-vā philosophy of reality).[14] Everything is held within the situation, the moment, creating patterns and dances through the rhythms of connection and separation. I feel this when I dance.

Part of the awareness of being present in the moment that dance offers is a sense that some things are other (other than me). Some things need to be unknown or beyond me in order for me to be dancing 'with' them. But rather than seeing this feeling as a justification to claim sovereignty over things and evidence that we are not all related, the worded-idea of CONNECTEDNESS/SEPARATEDNESS denotes that within everything there is an intra-connection of constant movement and rearrangement: a dance of Place.

All the colleagues with whom I worked during my fellowship felt that our making (and Place-making) had an impact through our awareness of connectedness and separatedness within the entirety of the lived experience. The pulse of when and what we connect with, and separate from, has an impact beyond what we can imagine, particularly on the ecology of the Earth, where urban populations can have a lasting and devastating impact on the organisms comprising the city with them.

---

12 Barad, *Meeting the Universe Halfway*.

13 Chipps, V. and S. Chiat (2003) *Pray from Your Heart: Teachings of a Lakota Elder*.

14 Ōkusitino Māhina discusses this most recently in Māhina,'Ō. (2021) 'Atamai-Loto, moe Faka'ofo'ofa-'Aonga: Tongan Tā-Vā Time-Space Philosophy of Mind–Heart and Beauty–Utility' [Special issue]. Pacific Studies, 44(1/2).

CONNECTEDNESS/SEPARATEDNESS marks the notion that all things are intra-connected, forming the contours of life. Demonstrated by the breathing organism of my dancing body, I am constantly involved in what enters my lungs as I breathe in, and I am part of what enters the world as I breathe out.

I assign CONNECTEDNESS/SEPARATEDNESS the element of the contour intervals (isolines) on the urban orienteering map. The contour intervals, indicating difference in elevation, are a way of showing the shape, the rise and fall of the land on an orienteering map. The contour intervals reflect how the movement of connection and separation gives a sense of configurations and formations within intra-connection. Through contour intervals, we become aware of a distinct moment, outlined by the ebb and flow of connectedness and separatedness.

CONNECTEDNESS/SEPARATEDNESS lifts experience off the fabric of consciousness, as land contours on a map lift the terrain off the fabric of the map. The rhythm and interruption of the pulse of CONNECTEDNESS/SEPARATEDNESS conjures response in the same way as the contour of a landscape evokes response. They both move us towards being able to recognise connections and separations in order to respond.

- CONNECTEDNESS/SEPARATEDNESS illustrates the multidimensionality of experience.
- CONNECTEDNESS/SEPARATEDNESS exposes the experience of the improvisation of the moment.
- CONNECTEDNESS/SEPARATEDNESS lifts experience off the fabric of consciousness into the realm of what is felt: un-camouflages habit, checks instinct and raises response into consciousness, giving it contours and nuance.

II. (AT LEAST) FOUR-DIMENSIONAL DISTANCE

The Parthenon is an object to a visitor and has so been for all the centuries since its construction. It is nevertheless an occurrence across some thousands of years. While for certain purposes of inquiry it may be marked off as object-in-environment, for thoroughgoing investigation it must be seized as situation, of which the object-specification is at best one phase or feature. – John Dewey.[15]

The worded-idea (AT LEAST) FOUR-DIMENSIONAL DISTANCE gives three-dimensional constructs of space at least one more dimension: the fourth dimension of time. This resonates with me, particularly in that it frames the notion that movement is a process or proposition across at least four dimensions. Thus, any creation (dance-choreography or building) is an event or movement which is both across space and across time.

I am in the car park of a Tesco supermarket. I move my right arm diagonally up and away from my body, reaching away towards the furthest corner of the tarmacked area where a red van is parked. I extend my hand and then my arm. I involve my shoulder and reach from my back. I shift my weight to one leg in order to reach even further. The movement in the situation of the car park is so different from the stretching of my arm in the situation of my house – my living room – where I have been isolating for the past month.

The stretch alters my breath. I feel the limits of my muscles in terms of the distance between where I am on the tarmac and where the red van is, and also the distance between when I was last outside in a large

15 Boydston, J. A. (ed.) (1989) *John Dewey: The Later Works, 1925–1953 (Vol. 16: 1949–1952, Essays, Typescripts, and Knowing and the Known)*, p. 69.

space and where I am now reaching from. Then, before I fall forward, I curve my arm back towards my chest. I bring my left arm to meet it, cradle-like. My weight moves towards my back leg, shifting from right to left. I curl myself in and see the ground just beneath me with small pebbles where the tarmac has cracked under the freezing of winters, and the warmth of summers, and the tyres of hundreds of cars. I reach back out towards the van. Reach out, curl in, reach out, curl in. I continue with this simple ten-minute dance. Reach out, curl in. The alarm on my phone rings at the ten-minute mark, and I stop the dance. I am surprised when the alarm sounds. I feel slightly disorientated because of the repetition of the movement. Time seems to wrap itself around the repetition of my movement. The sense of how big the space is (the nature of my reaching), how fast the ten minutes go by, becomes the condition of my moving body. The dance movement filters the size of the car park and the size of the ten minutes. The movement of my body is the filter through which the comprehension of being in the spatial-temporality of the car park is deciphered. My dance movement becomes the method of perception of the time and space of the car park in the moment of the ten minutes.

(AT LEAST) FOUR-DIMENSIONAL DISTANCE recognises that movement measures distance in both time and space. Thus, when we design movement (around the city), we reconfigure and shape both time and space. For embodied beings, time has to be located in a space, just as space has to be located in a time. Movement (including stillness) is a method that can be used to notice the measurements of (AT LEAST) FOUR-DIMENSIONAL DISTANCE. I see movement as a method – as a mechanism – for being aware of, researching in or experiencing (AT LEAST) FOUR-DIMENSIONAL DISTANCE.

I wonder if it is possible that (AT LEAST) FOUR-DIMENSIONAL DISTANCE becomes a Place through the movement of CONNECTEDNESS/SEPARATEDNESS. This leads me to see dance movement as a method for noticing the expansion of space and/or time and thus as a tool for understanding spatial practices.

I assign (AT LEAST) FOUR-DIMENSIONAL DISTANCE the element of grid lines. The grid lines on an orienteering map allow the reader to locate a particular place. But the grid lines, as a human, superimposed mechanism on the landscape, are not constant. They are all contingent and operate to help calculate distance in terms of a shifting position. If (AT LEAST) FOUR-DIMENSIONAL DISTANCE allows us to notice, and navigate through, space and time, the same task is given to the grid lines on an orienteering map.

- (AT LEAST) FOUR-DIMENSIONAL DISTANCE contextualises movement (and experience) in the same way grid lines contextualise a map.
- (AT LEAST) FOUR-DIMENSIONAL DISTANCE underscores locatable moments of consciousness: moments when dancing makes one more conscious of being in a Place.
- (AT LEAST) FOUR-DIMENSIONAL DISTANCE locates moments of experience, allowing them to be recallable.

III. AGENCY

The sharp cold of a breeze caught on the eddies of a passing boat leads me to take a gasp. My quick in-breath alters my weight as the small pebbles under my toes rearrange beneath my bending knee. Pebbles chatter in their movement on the slope of the shore, within the limits imposed by the concrete girder that is dug deep into the sand, preventing the pebbles from rumbling down the beach and away from the pressure of my toes. My intention is to balance on my left leg, lifting my right leg up behind me. The teeter between the toes and stones provokes the *classicism* of the muscles in my upper back to throw my right arm back behind in an arabesque balance. Arabesqued, my spine takes the vibration of the pebbles from my standing leg. The fabric of my sweater pulls its threads of yellow wool tightly across my chest as my arm extends behind me. And as my ankle recalibrates with the settling of the stones, my wrist is revealed while the sweater exposes the part of my skin it can no longer conceal. The chill of the cool December air pricks the blood coursing through the veins of my wrist, and I become aware of the faint warmth provided by the concrete girder's absorption of sun. Concrete sings with moist algae, tormented with whispers of deep ocean liners and rust, as the tide floods in twice a day. With its potholes mended by the caress of emerald sea moss, the girder offers to leave the green history of this moment on the yellow of my sweater, should I allow my weight to succumb to the rabble of the pebbles and give up on my balancing leg. In return, I mark the girder with the sharp shadow of my arm, back, and outstretched leg. We are for a moment. Then I breathe out, skin on the back of my outstretched hand confesses the fleeting temptation of the familiar arabesque, and my stomach draws my leg into rearranging more pebbles as I step forward.

Reflecting on the moment of dancing on the shoreline in the city, I experience a moment of a breath in and out that exemplifies the worded-idea of AGENCY. That moment was organised in the experience of dance that happened out of the agencies of the slope of the shore, the pebbles, the concrete girder, the angle of the sun, the fabric of my clothing and my muscles. These multiple agencies came together in a moment I experienced as dance.

They were informed by the histories that had come before that moment (the tide that had gone out, the warming of my muscles during a bike ride that had taken me there) and futures to come (my cold fingers becoming numb, the tide's return, the pebbles' slow drift along the shore). Dancing on the shore in the city captured the whole connected community of *us* at that moment, and the separateness of the agencies of the elements that created the togetherness of that moment.

AGENCY is an acknowledgement that everything has its own future. Dancing with the premise of AGENCY involves a sense of the edges of oneself, which, in turn, brings attention to the flux of everything, the pulse of CONNECTEDNESS/SEPARATEDNESS and (AT LEAST) FOUR-DIMENSIONAL DISTANCE in movement. Following ideas put forward by René Descartes – *I think there for I am* – in the West, movement and change is equated with uncertainty, and uncertainty with a questioning of our own existence. I suggest that uncertainty is merely the awareness of the pulse of change that is CONNECTEDNESS/SEPARATEDNESS. If everything is in the pulse of changing connection and separation, then within a place there is a multiplicity of futures, and thus agencies. I assign this idea of AGENCY the element of road junctions. A road junction reflects AGENCY in that it negotiates many movements and directions coming together and/or separating.

- AGENCY influences where one moves from and to, indicates points to begin from or perceived distance from.
- AGENCY is the ability to make choices about the direction/change of movement and the awareness of the impact of direction and distance on what one perceives to be other than oneself.
- AGENCY involves the direction of movement and the ability to use movement to conjure distance.

IV. GROWTH

Although the October air is chilly, the midday sunshine creates the sum of my body as a crumpled, circular shadow around my feet. I stand on the pavement and look down at the spill of my shadow self on to the paving stones beneath my ballet shoes. The thin fabric of the canvas ballet shoes discloses the unevenness of the seams of concrete holding the paving slabs together. I stand in the centre of a paving stone, filling the square shape with my feet and the silhouette of my shadow. From this island my eyes trace a path to the next paving stone, then to the next and the next. Avoiding the seams between slabs, I leap between the stones, while my shadow slightly expands at the height of my jump and shrinks back down to meet my feet as I land. Each leap and pulse of the expanding shadow is a unique experience of momentary flight.

As I bob from stone to stone, I make a pattern: sometimes extending my leg out in front of me to bend forward; sometimes extending my leg to the side to skip sideways; sometimes stretching backward or diagonally; sometimes making a half turn to watch my shadow twist and re-form at my feet. The directions of my leap-dance respond to the paving stones. I try not to step on the rough seams between them. Then, I respond to the cracks across them, trying to only dance where the paving stone is fractured. Later, I try to avoid these veins. There are moments when my dance takes me close to the edge of the pavement, where it meets a building. I need to curve my back and swivel as I land to avoid grazing my shoulder on the rough bricks of the building's edge.

My leap reshapes again when a square of the pavement is occupied by a discarded sweet wrapper. I contort my landing to avoid slipping on the litter. I notice more opportunity for movement as I play with the shape of my shadow-self meeting the shadow of another, such as a long spiky line cast by a small tree growing at the pavement's edge. This playfulness becomes a dialogue in movement, with the continuity of each jump-step constructing the form of my leaps.

As my back curves away from the threat of grazing the wall, I open my arms and see the shadow of my extended arm trail my presence across three paving stones at once. This time, before I leap again, I extend my left arm and right leg, spreading myself and my shadow self across five paving stones. The momentum of my leaps and my outstretched body consumes paving stones. I leap sideways holding an extended star shape. This connects the five paving stones from which my leap began with four further ones as my extended left shadow arm spills, flooding the pavement all the way to the edge of a blue rubbish bag which lies outside a doorway. I start to build a relationship with the wall structures and litter and other unique elements of the pavement as the dance grows forward, sideways, and backward along the paving stones.

GROWTH could be considered in terms of philosopher John Dewey's notion of continuity: the passage of continuity of experiences.[16] I suggest that GROWTH is not about getting bigger in a measurable way. Rather, GROWTH is revealed through the continuity of experiences: the connections between them and their cumulative nature. Thus, GROWTH is recognised through the transactional nature of the situation and determined by the continuity of experience that the assemblage of elements in a situation accumulate (and not through a universal measurement of size).

16 Hildebrand, D. (2008) *Dewey: A Beginner's Guide.*

As I dance, my physical impulses instigate the movement of my body. For instance, as I take a step on the pebbles on the shore of the river, the leg I am balancing on readjusts to the movement of the pebbles while I tip my weight onto the other leg. The next time I encounter the AGENCY of the moving pebbles underfoot, my body connects the previous experience on the beach with this new encounter with pebbles, and this continuity of experience is what I see as GROWTH. Similarly, the movement of turning in a pirouette relies on the continuity of memories of past experiences of that movement.

When I think about an element for GROWTH within the city, the mosaic web of continuity that paving stones create resonates. I give GROWTH the element of paving stones on the urban orienteering map.

- GROWTH mosaics into distinguishable structures or ideas.
- The continuity of GROWTH influences movement in and out of structures and relationships.
- The continuity of GROWTH generates a sense of accumulation.

V. POWER (OVER, TO, PLACE)

Dancing again, on a pedestrian refuge island in King's Cross: I keep the rhythm of the beat of my heart with my feet, lifting one heel and then the other, kneading catlike on the concrete island of the road crossing. The small bones of my feet caress the concrete only centimetres away from the assault of traffic hurtling down the roads on either side of me. The roads around King's Cross bleed into my history as a dancer. I have been coming to the King's Cross area to take dance classes from the age of eleven. I began dancing in an after-school club

nearby, and throughout my early teens, I took part in contact improvisation jams in empty warehouses above the canal that are now expensive condominiums. In adulthood, I have given classes and lectures in the theatres and colleges in the new buildings along the canal. I knead these memories together as I move my feet into the concrete of the traffic island in rhythm with the beating of my heart. As a car passes, very close, very fast, daring me to fall, I focus on the sides of the buildings in front of me to keep myself steady. I can see myself across the ages when I look at the wall of the blocks that line the streets here. I know where this part of the city hides its memories. I am revealed in the layers of brick beneath the paving and along the canal.

My movements have a confidence despite or because of the heaviness of the busy roads around me: I recognise myself here. I know here through myself; I know when it will rain by the smell of the air. I grew up here. I am of this place. As I start to shape my arms slowly – a counter movement to the beat I am keeping with my feet – I read the air with the curves and spikes of my fingers. I follow the implications of the wind and know where to find the sun. My feet pulse, lifting one heel and then the other, as my arms reach out in a slow manifestation of the throb around me. I dance to the noise of the traffic, to the cars panting at the red lights, to the vans rattling past me on the green lights. I feel my permanence while moving on the traffic island. I dance with how these streets possess my history and frame my future. With arms constantly reshaping, my fingers alive, my toes in rhythm and outstretched, one or two single drops of rain marking the concrete beneath me, I breathe in the power of this Place.

There were three expressions of the idea of POWER I explored as part of the Navigations period of my fellowship. The first two emerged through a series of conversations with engineer and dancer Ellie Cosgrave about womanhood. She talked about power over something and power to do something. Here I adapt these concepts to challenge the Western capitalist frameworks that seem to value POWER (OVER) and POWER (TO) as different expressions of AGENCY within the city.

POWER (OVER) denotes POWER that directs the relationship one has with something and also other people's relationships with that thing. Making a piece of choreography, or a building, requires resources over which we have POWER. This gives us the ability – POWER – to realise a trajectory and to manifest an artifact from our creative process. To explore POWER (OVER) in the lexicon, I suggest different nuances within POWER through the process of making:

1   the POWER over the movement trajectory to make something;
2   the POWER over the movement trajectory *others* will encounter with what is being made;
3   the POWER over determination of what relationships *others* will have with the movement trajectory of what is being made.

In the making process, success often lies in how well the maker is able to limit the relationship others have with the thing made. POWER (OVER) implies that it is crucial to the success of making something that any experiencer of the thing will have a similar relationship with it as the one the maker imagined they would have.

POWER (TO) is not a solution to POWER (OVER). POWER (TO) magnifies where POWER (OVER) is present in a situation. That is, if I have POWER (TO) do something, it usually means I have POWER (OVER) something to facilitate my POWER (TO) do. POWER (TO) can

be used as a rudder to notice POWER (OVER). The third expression of POWER – POWER (PLACE) – draws on the conversations with Scott L. Pratt and Gediminas Urbonas as part of the MIT podcast series *Choreographing the City* (2020).[17] Scott discussed North American frameworks of epistemology, particularly the concepts of power in Vine Deloria Jr and Daniel R. Wildcat's book *Power and Place*, published in 2001.

This third exploration of POWER involves the way one realises oneself through being of the moment, drawing on knowledges, meaning and understanding through the somatic response to Place.

POWER (PLACE) is informed by the web or network of agencies that is a particular Place. POWER (PLACE) offers the energy and opportunity for GROWTH and CONNECTEDNESS/SEPARATEDNESS: the POWER of being *a part of it all*.

POWER (OVER), POWER (TO), POWER (PLACE): across all these nuances of POWER, there is a shared engagement with the accessibility of the freedom of movement (movement needed to make, to have an intention, to grow). Because of this, I assigned POWER the elements of railway lines and main roads on the map. I see POWER as providing the infrastructure for energetic and controlled movement with a directed intention.

- POWER has attributes of high velocity and directional movement.
- POWER affects points of perception: where one moves from and to.
- POWER becomes an invisible or unperceived actor determining connections, actions and relationships.

17 Akinleye, A. and G. Urbonas (2021) 'Episode Six: Agency and the Demonic', *Choreographing the City*. ACT, MIT. [Podcast]. Available at: https://player.fm/series/3311938.

VI. RESISTANCE

I need the resistance of the floor to dance. Every time I jump or balance or step, I negotiate the fragility of my bones and muscles with gravitational RESISTANCE. This is not resistance in political terms, such as responding to an injustice. I am considering RESISTANCE in terms of rigour. If I jump on a soft floor, hard floor, sprung dance floor, all these conditions offer different resistances. I need the rigour of practice on these different kinds of floor resistances to develop techniques that can facilitate the movement I want to make. The RESISTANCE forces me into the rigour of noticing beyond my intention and makes me re-evaluate how I can engage with my intention within the conditions of the situation.

However, I acknowledge that rigour has been used as an excuse to defend injustices. For instance, gatekeeping in dance (or academia) has been justified in the guise of seeking rigour, when those excluded would argue it was unjust protectionism. But here, in relation to the other worded-ideas, RESISTANCE is where rigour leads to GROWTH (and the continuity of the pulse of CONNECTEDNESS/SEPARATEDNESS).

In conversations as part of the *Choreographing the City* podcast series (2020), social scientist and founder of Theatrum Mundi, Richard Sennett, and choreographer Liz Lerman both separately mentioned RESISTANCE in relation to artistic growth.[18] They discussed how, as one becomes more involved in the choreographic activity, informed by processes of trial and error, RESISTANCE is useful in the rigour of creative exploration. Over time, in the process of creative exploration, the choreographer makes the material more familiar to them, and thus they encounter less resistance because of this familiarity. This can raise an issue of accessibility because as the material becomes more familiar to the choreographer, it can become more obtuse for someone who is newly encountering it. RESISTANCE accentuates the correlation between familiarity and accessibility in making. In Place-making (such as choreographing), the more familiar the maker is with the materials and concepts they are creating with, the more risk there is of making the Place inaccessible to people unlike themselves. As I choreograph, I use RESISTANCE as a 'visitor' to my own ideas. I think about the role of RESISTANCE as I start to devise movement. I keep asking myself how I locate the movement I am working with: Does it have a familiar sensation; do I recognise where it is rooted from? How accessible is the movement and how much am I creating what I feel comfortable doing out of habit? What changes if I engage with a floor or music as elements to resist?

RESISTANCE acknowledges AGENCY and influences GROWTH (creates or disrupts continuities). Within the experience of RESISTANCE, there is a realisation of impact, encounter, presence, now-ness. A loud sound, an overpowering smell, a locked door can all provide RESISTANCE, shifting the felt sense or focus of Place. RESISTANCE provides us with information within Place, through giving experience a vivid sense of encounter. RESISTANCE is an encounter tempered by the diffraction of familiarity and/or accessibility. It provides the parameter through which we experience. I assign RESISTANCE the element of the map key.

- RESISTANCE determines the parameters of what one is working with.
- RESISTANCE spotlights the layers of limitations.

18 Akinleye and Urbonas (2021) 'Episode Three: Resistance and Double-Barrelled Aspiration' and 'Episode Eight: Into Motion', *Choreographing the City*.

- RESISTANCE shapes understanding of encounter and can be used to confirm presence.

VII. BOUNDARY

There is a small river that runs alongside the road I take en route to the train station. It is called Salmon Brook. Maybe once its name described the characteristic of the brook, but now the name is an optimistic desire for its future. On dry weeks, it trickles along a few meters below the road level. I look down at it as I hurry across the road to the station. But when it is raining, the small stream thunders past me faster than my hurried footfall. There is always litter in the stream: discarded coffee cups, plastic bottles, broken umbrellas; the flotsam and jetsam of the city.

Once, after a heavy storm, I notice a shopping trolley wedged into the slight curve of the riverbank. It sticks out into the centre of the stream. The water rushes through its metal frame, creating a weir in the current where a football has become caught in the temporary BOUNDARY the trolly creates. Water pouring through the trolley's frame torments the stuck ball, making it spin and revolve.

Inspired by the ball, I plant my right foot on the ground in front of my left, bend both my knees and push off my back (left) foot, rotating around on my front (right) foot. I repeat, lifting my left leg up to bring my foot to my right knee: turning in a pirouette. As soon as my revolution ends, I steady myself by touching my left toes back on the ground but only for long enough to push myself off again into a new whirl. I try to keep up with the rhythm of the rotations of the ball. The spinning necessitates that I use all the momentum that my hips, shoulders and

back can produce. The transitions between the end of one rotation and the beginning of a new one define each new turn, which is unique and shaped by the last position the momentum shaped me into. Each turn has a culmination, a BOUNDARY, where the shape of my rotating body holds a distinct form to complete that rotation. Then, I feel a shift, as each new turn emerges from my spinning, and my body falls into a new turning propulsion. The BOUNDARY of one turn thus determines the distinction of the next. I notice that my spinning evolves into a sense of porousness as the BOUNDARY to each turn is brought about by the last.

I try again the BOUNDARY dance, which empathises with the distinct rhythm of the movement created out of the situation of the entanglements of the ball, rainwater, rotation, shopping trolley and walk to the station. This time I find a different kind of stream, a stream of traffic, to see if I can experience the same distinction of one distinct boundary (movement) affecting the next.

I stand on the edge of the road, within a square in front of a train station. I watch the traffic stream past, then a plastic bag catches my eye. It is wide open, snaring the air as it gets thrown up by the motion of a passing car. It looks like a skyborne jellyfish, pumping itself wide as the air captures it and hurls it above the cars. Then, it flutters down deflated, only to be cast upward again by the next car.

Later, alone in my living room, I attempt to empathise with the pattern and rhythm of the plastic bag caught in the eddies of the stream of traffic. I trace an upward, swelling, broadening movement with my hand that extends into my shoulder and down my body to the tips of my toes. Then, I drop down, bending my knees and twisting my hand behind me. I chase my fingers with my eyes, and this movement spins me round. I remember how the bag was kicked upward by the passing current of cars. I spring from my bent knee to lift to my right elbow on the tide of empathic memory. The bony corner of my bent arm makes a curving swipe, bringing me onto the toes of my left foot. The rest of my body hangs from the arch of my elbow, which is already descending towards my waist. Another breath, and this time I hike my hip to catch the tide of remembered traffic and the bag's next ascent. My movements oscillate to the pulsation of the remembered current of traffic.

BOUNDARY in this lexicon is not about demarcations of difference or sameness. Rather, BOUNDARY is the manifestation of a particular phenomenon or distinctiveness: BOUNDARY is an acknowledgement that through the responsiveness, transaction, or intra-action, the situation produces something distinctive, something with a periphery, contingent on that particular entanglement of Place. Through intra-action BOUNDARIES emerge.

At the moment of its emergence, BOUNDARY marks the edge of something distinct and is uncrossable, but it is also temporary through being contingent on the rhythm and flow of movement within the intra-action of things. This means that a BOUNDARY exists within the temporal, spatial movement of CONNECTEDNESS/SEPARATEDNESS. Thus, although BOUNDARY is uncrossable when it emerges, it is also temporary and contingent on the particular manifestation of meaning in the moment that produces awareness of it.

Because BOUNDARY is a moving and shifting flow, which manifests through the meaning made of ever-changing assemblages, I have assigned it the element of stream on the map. This could be a stream of water or a stream of traffic.

- BOUNDARY creates distinctive flow of movement.
- BOUNDARY manages the flow of a structure or moment.
- BOUNDARY appears to distort direction because of the flows of movement it temporarily creates.

VIII. PRECISENESS

There is a wall in front of me that I want to climb. It is not that high, but it is quite narrow. I first place my hands on its top and slide my right knee onto it, pressing my skin to its bricks warmed by the late August sun. Leaning on the palms of my hands, I hoist my other leg up. From there, I can carefully stand up. As I stand atop the wall, I feel a level of accomplishment. The wall allows me to swing my leg in a circular pattern, balancing along the edge of the top of the wall. I stretch my arms out, fingertips hovering in space on either side of me. Everything looks different up here, but I find balancing along the edge of the wall limiting. My dance steps are consumed with maintaining the preciseness of the movement along the narrow surface of the wall, with no option for a sidestep. In the meticulousness of this one-directional dance the wall and I are creating, it is difficult to retrace my movement backward. Then I miss a step and come off the wall onto the grass. I realise that my original careful ascent masked the possibilities my clumsy fall opened up. There is a whole new set of movements I can start to explore.

The fall off the wall and the climb back onto the wall open up a new choreography that allows me to resist by moving along the length of the wall. The step up onto the top of the wall is quite high and relies on the strength of my thigh to haul the rest of my body up. So, instead, I start to play with using my hips to sit on the edge of the wall and propel myself forward from the sitting position by using my hands to push myself off the edge of the wall. Then, I turn to swing my hands forward and catch myself falling off the wall. I add a kick sideways to allow my leg to lie against the ledge of the wall. My dance takes me along the length of the wall. Each time I step off, I am unsure of what I will be stepping down onto. Engaging with the wall dance involves moments of stepping into the invisible or unseen areas the wall conceals and traverses. Each time I step across or over the wall, there is a sensation of falling that elongates the moment, as if the unknown thickens the now-ness of the step.

In dance, architecture or engineering, preciseness codifies actions undertaken to avoid physical, financial, or social outcomes that are unwanted or deemed impossible. PRECISENESS guides us – choreographers, dancers, architects and engineers – in the process towards achieving the virtuosity of a dance step or the beauty of a building. Through PRECISENESS, we can avoid engaging with the unwanted. Through PRECISENESS, we can avoid engaging with what we have judged or presumed impossible. There is also a danger that what is unwanted is conflated with the impossible.

During a conversation over Zoom with Ellie Cosgrave, we exchanged stories from our late teens about incidents that led to the induction into our respective fields: Ellie into engineering and me into dance. As a teenager on a work experience, Ellie went to see a pier on the Thames, and the engineer who had designed it said that it was impossible to make it wheelchair accessible at low tide. She was immediately excited by the challenge and came up with some solutions that could work. The engineer said, 'Well, that's interesting but impossible.' Later, as Ellie explained her ideas again to the engineer, he said, 'No, you can't do that. It's too expensive.'

In return, I told Ellie a story of my nineteen-year-old self, finishing my pre-professional training in ballet. At the end of the three years of training, my class had an interview with our teachers to support us in thinking about what dance companies to contact to start auditioning to begin our careers. I was told it was impossible for Black bodies to be precise enough to be employed in dancing ballet (in Britain).

In both our stories, the worlds we wanted to begin careers in used PRECISENESS as the mechanism for corralling the constraints needed to protect us from the impossible. And PRECISENESS was used to mask the unwanted as impossible. The value of the transdisciplinary approach to Place-making in our collaborations is that we can start to interrogate our own and each other's use of PRECISENESS.

As an element on the urban orienteering map, I assigned PRECISENESS walls and fences, which act as organisers of movement by being the guiding, directional and even controlling elements of the city.

- PRECISENESS is the rules or regulations one can go along with, follow, but also fall off, step across and over.
- PRECISENESS can create invisible or unperceived actors in interactions.
- PRECISENESS influences connections across the shape of now.

IX. IMPROVISATION

As a choreographer, I do not attempt to predict the future experience of the audience but instead try to offer a framework of movement for the dance performers to be responsive within as dance. The art of choreography is that the dancer is always in dialogue with the moment. In conversation with the renowned choreographer Dianne McIntyre for the monograph *Dance, Architecture and Engineering*, Dianne spoke about her choreography in terms of creating *spontaneous composition*,[19] which acknowledges the importance of the dance work to being alive, by being responsive to the assemblage of the moment. Dianne's term *spontaneous composition* underlines the informed dialogue and responsiveness of IMPROVISATION. IMPROVISATION is, as architect David Adjaye articulates, 'a free form dialogue, [for instance] where El Anatsui sets up scenarios. ... Improvisation is a force to be mastered, like Coltrane talks about, so that it flows through the idea of making'.[20]

Thus, IMPROVISATION can be a way to articulate the crucial role of response in Place-making. When we, Place-makers, create through design or choreography, we inevitably change the nature of the elements we draw together within Place. However, as organisers and makers, we cannot predict the future of the assemblages we initiate. The making process becomes the note from which those assemblages riff.

During Navigations, my collaborators and I were interested in how we could weave *response-iveness*, *response-ability*, and being *response-able* into our creating. IMPROVISATION is the route response takes, understanding and allowing for multiple relationships and rhythms, connections and separations. IMPROVISATION in the lexicon is the ongoing, heightened awareness of possibility.

Since more than one thing happens at once in any (AT LEAST) FOUR-DIMENSIONAL

DISTANCE, IMPROVISATION can move through space and time, skip across or dive into the multiple roots/routes of a moment. I assign IMPROVISATION the element of any given route across the urban orienteering map.

- IMPROVISATION is a contingent, temporary, responsive dialogue.
- IMPROVISATION constantly creates structures in itself that can then be deviated from.
- IMPROVISATION belongs to the multifaceted shape of the moment.

X. SCORE

Score can refer to a notation such as a musical score, but it also means to achieve, attain, do, mark, record, count. Within the lexicon, I suggest that this word has a meaning across all its subtle iterations. In this sense, the Navigations research is about scoring the moment: creating a temporary infrastructure for understanding things, a navigation for being present. I see SCORE as an infrastructure rather than a set of instructions. Dance, or music, or a building are realisable to us through the assemblage (the situation) that reveals them.

In a conversation recorded for the podcast *Silence and Stillness* (published by Theatrum Mundi in September 2020), in reference to a music sheet or the steps of a set dance to a specific piece of music, I and author, social scientist, and musician Richard Sennett wondered if the dance or music is in the steps and notes on the paper or in the gaps between those steps and notes.[21]

---

19 Akinleye (2021) *Dance, Architecture and Engineering*, p. 131.

20 Adjaye, D. (2020) 'Lecture by David Adjaye on El Anatsui'. Haus der Kunst. 8 July 2020. Available at: https://www.youtube.com/watch?v=bQA3yUnZHcs.

21 Cetrulo, A. (2020) *Silence and Stillness*. [Podcast]. 10 September 2020. Available at: https://theatrum-mundi.org/live/silence-and-stillness/; Karimnia, E. and F. Kostourou (eds.) (2021) *Embodying Otherness*.

The answer to this depends on how one values the dancer's or musician's technique, virtuosity, interpretation and/or experience in terms of the number of times they have danced or played the notated piece. If one answers that the dance or music is in the steps or notes – that one values the technique and virtuosity of the performer to reproduce perfect examples of what is notated – then the score becomes a set of instructions. If one suggests that the dance or music is in the spaces between the steps or notes – that one values the performer's interpretation and experience – then the score becomes infrastructure.

Positioning SCORE as a set of instructions raises questions around POWER and AGENCY within practice. It assumes a shared reality: it assumes that those reading the instructions will interpret them in a very similar way to the person who wrote them. In other words, SCORE as instructions works to confirm a similar shared outcome.

But I am more attracted to SCORE as infrastructure. This means that SCORE offers a framework within which a set of knowledges or experiences can be revealed. Places can become SCORES: infrastructures holding moments of IMPROVISATION. I wonder if this quality of places is at the heart of what it means to *belong*, which I understand as the awareness of one's AGENCY in the choreography of the spontaneous composition of the moment. The moment is ever changing, and thus SCORE is the container where IMPROVISATION can happen. I assigned SCORE the element of the substance of the urban orienteering map, for instance, the paper a map is printed on.

- SCORE is a temporary infrastructure for understanding things.
- SCORE is a method for recalling structures or responses.
- SCORE is an apparatus for recording or settling a moment.

Continued Steps with the Lexicon

My local London streets had been my partner in exploring the worded-ideas. Through reflecting on what elements to assign to the worded-ideas on an urban orienteering map, and the site-specific moments of choreography, the city brought up questions about the way knowledges from dance can contribute to developing awareness of the ability to be responsive to the city environment. In the streets of London, dancing the lexicon brought about a sensitivity to the everyday dance of responsiveness that is a key part of the process of Place-making.

The plotting of the lexicon onto the London streets around me had become an ethical composition: the choreography of the city; the choreography of being with what was around me; the choreography of enquiring into how to be present with the city and all its elements. My thinking, responding, and meaning-making merged through the opportunities for dance that exploring my local streets as a metaphor for elements of the lexicon offered. As I worked with and through the worded-ideas, the lexicon introduced intriguing questions about the human capacity to conceive of Place. The worded-ideas offered an insight into the shaping of body and city. The material practice of dancing the lexicon with the objects around me involved foregrounding meaning in the soma of shapes, feelings, and memories. I was reminded of the premise about body and city shaping each other, with which I started the fellowship. The next step of Navigations was to focus on the relationships – or routes – that could be created through the plotted lexicon.

ADVENTURES

03

to ramble	to respond
to chance	to undertake

In early 2021, I caught Covid-19, which developed into long Covid. The first half of 2021 thus meant for me a drawn-out recovery process, with weeks in bed followed by months regaining the energy to leave my house. From my bed, I took myself on mental walks around cities. I saw each walk as a form of choreography, choreographing my journey around my memories. As I started to recover, the mental walks became short physical walks around my local London streets. After being unable to leave the house for such a long time, each walk became an event, an opportunity to explore, and an invitation to continue to engage with the worded-ideas. I focused on my local streets to explore the lexicon through everyday occurrences. In the process of exploration, I drew on the now-ness – the present-ness – of dance to establish a sense of being physically, mentally, and ethically in the *moment* of the street. Playing on the ideas of the Situationist International,[22] I mischievously called my dance-walks *moment-ist walks*. I documented the progression of the *moment-ist* walks through three prompts: encountering the moment, presence within the moment, and emergent properties of the moment.

Here, I offer these prompts and the principles of the moment-ist walks as an exercise you, the reader, might like to embark upon. Below, I briefly share my reflections collected while undertaking a series of these walks in 2021. Please note that I have no fixed outcomes to share or results to report.

On my moment-ist walks, the symbolic locations of the lexicon within the city became choices of awareness, witnessing, marking, and being present and responsive within the physical and metaphysical elements around me. The walks became tools that led to uncovering logics of the accumulation of the city, and the meaning of being a citizen of a particular city (London), through the moments of encounter with the elements of the lexicon. This exploration gave me coordinates to belong to the moment through my response to the meaning-making of the city in those Places. The moment-ist dance-walks suggested playful movements for exploring body as the apparatus for spontaneous composition, the apparatus for thinking with and thinking through. As body and city shaped each other to fit into the narrative of being present in the street, I reflected on the changing sense of presence: the muscles, breath and thoughts changed as I responded to the moment and was present together with all that was around me. I found that the walks helped me notice my responsiveness to the moment of everyday encounter: how I was a part within the spontaneous composition of the city.

22 A radical movement of the mid-twentieth century devoted to the disruption and reimagining of the systems that govern everyday life.

Navigation One: Encountering the Moment

The first prompt asks you to pre-plan a walk to a destination (a shop, for instance). Notice where the elements of the city assigned to the worded-ideas intersect on your route. This will provide a starting point to explore the lexicon through the meaning-making of the city's streets. For example: during one moment-ist walk's route, the paving stones (GROWTH) come to the edge of a main road (POWER). Thus, within the meaning-making of the physicality of the moment-ist walk, GROWTH meets POWER, igniting thinking about the relationship between GROWTH and POWER through the physical framing of the city's design.

When I began exploring the worded-ideas, dancing in the urban setting was a thinking tool for me. I was focused on the meaning-making that practice was revealing. The movement was providing me with reflections on how the worded-ideas were in conceptual relationships with each other. Those reflections were embodied but perhaps more theoretical in their nature.

That body – my pre-Covid body – did not have to pay any attention to the strength, stamina and practised skill required to perform the dance movements. Post-Covid, my easily exhausted body emphasised the relationships between the worded-ideas through the physicality of engaging with the elements of the city as I undertook the moment-ist walks. For example, the shortness of breath revealed the length of the pavement, the strength I needed to step onto a wall reflected on the toll of PRECISENESS, and the size of the paving stones left me reflecting on GROWTH.

I noticed that the lexicon started to produce meaning in response to a constellation of choices and relationships between and across the worded-ideas and streets. This network of meaning allowed me to be reflectively enfolded in the emerging relationships of the worded-ideas in the same way as I was physically enfolded in the network of the city's streets.

Navigation One
Map Key

CONNECTEDNESS/SEPARATEDNESS:
The contour intervals on the map
- illustrates the multidimensionality of experience

(AT LEAST) FOUR-DIMENSIONAL DISTANCE:
The grid lines
- contextualises movement (and experience) in the
  same way the grid lines contextualise a map

AGENCY: *Road junctions*
- influences where one moves from and to, indicates
  points to begin from or perceived distance from

GROWTH: *Paving stones*
- mosaics into distinguishable structures
  or ideas

POWER: *Railway lines and/or main roads*
- has attributes of high velocity and directional
  movement

RESISTANCE: *The key to the map*
- determines the parameters of what one is working
  with

BOUNDARY: *Rivers or streams (water or traffic)*
- creates distinctive flow of movement

PRECISENESS: *Walls and fences*
- is the rules or regulations one can go along with,
  follow, but also fall off, step across and over

IMPROVISATION: *The route (at any given moment)*
- is a contingent, temporary, responsive dialogue

SCORE: *The substance of the map*
- is a temporary infrastructure for understanding
  things

Navigation Two: Presence within the Moment

The second prompt asks you to begin a walk to a destination (a shop, for instance). Again, notice where the elements of the city assigned to the worded-ideas intersect. In this prompt, you can choose how you engage with the design of the street at the intersection of the worded-ideas, but you must reach your original, intended destination. For instance, during one moment-ist walk's route, the paving stones (GROWTH) come to the edge of a main road (POWER). Thus, within the meaning-making of the physicality of the moment-ist walk, GROWTH meets POWER. In the first prompt, I cross the road to keep on my planned route (I accept the process of my GROWTH element being interrupted by the POWER element). Within the conditions of this second prompt, I choose to use the trajectory of POWER to give the direction to my GROWTH but not cross it. Thus, I do not cross the road. I follow the paving stones around a corner along the main road. However, because there is a pre-determined destination – the shop – I have to compromise on how I engage with the city's elements to still get to the shop. I reflect on what these compromises are through the framing of the design of this city. Does the city expect me to always be willing to compromise my GROWTH to POWER in order to arrive?

As the moment-ist walks continued, I was fascinated by the oscillating distances in meaning created between the verbal language of the worded-ideas and the somatic landscape of my choices. The moment-ist walks used the city as a partner. The streets framed the unexpected, multiple agencies and the logics of their coming together. For instance, turning a street corner and finding where a wall (PRECISENESS) once stood now lay paving stones (GROWTH) with a car left askew to the stream of traffic (BOUNDARY), its front crumpled and airbag slumped on the front seat. This was an unexpected combination of PRECISENESS, GROWTH and BOUNDARY to which I had to physically respond in my walk. The moment-ist walks' process of navigating the worded-ideas highlighted the notion of response as the unique logic that emerges from the moment of us-ness the city frames.

I also noticed how memory can become an almost tangible somatic experience at some points in the walks. For instance, the place where a rat ran across the pavement in front of me started to be a location I avoided, even if it meant I had to take an indirect route. The rat-pavement memory informed how I engaged with GROWTH in that area. It felt as tangible a factor in where I chose to walk as a physical building. I started to feel my presence in the streets as a rich, layered tapestry of responses and choices.

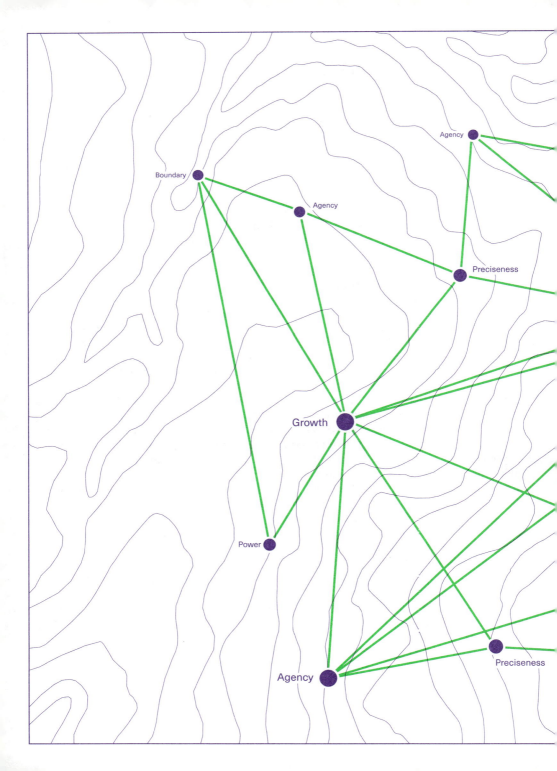

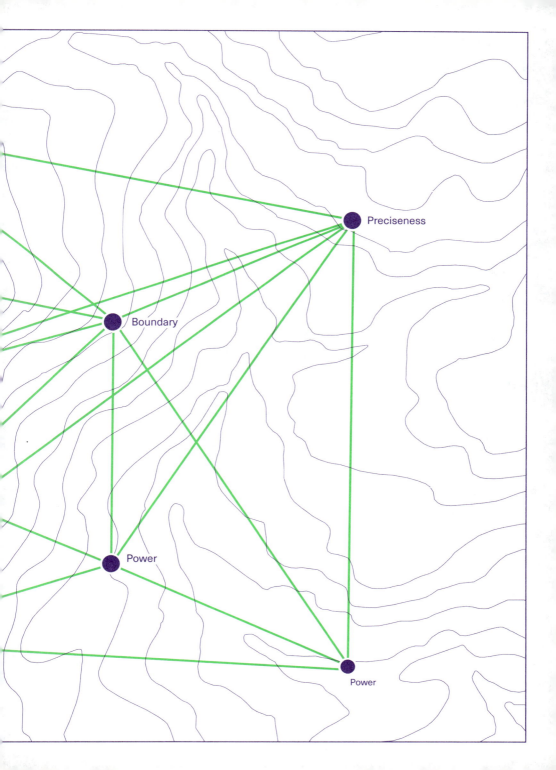

Navigation Two
Map Key

CONNECTEDNESS/SEPARATEDNESS:
The contour intervals on the map
- illustrates the multidimensionality of experience
- exposes the experience of the improvisation of the moment

(AT LEAST) FOUR-DIMENSIONAL DISTANCE:
The grid lines
- contextualises movement (and experience) in the same way the grid lines contextualise a map
- underscores locatable moments of consciousness: moments when dancing makes one more conscious of being in a Place

AGENCY: *Road junctions*
- influences where one moves from and to, indicates points to begin from or perceived distance from
- is the ability to make choices about the direction/ change of movement and the awareness of the impact of direction and distance on what one perceives to be other than oneself

GROWTH: *Paving stones*
- mosaics into distinguishable structures or ideas
- influences movement in and out of structures and relationships

POWER: *Railway lines and/or main roads*
- has attributes of high velocity and directional movement
- affects points of perception: where one moves from and to

RESISTANCE: *The key to the map*
- determines the parameters of what one is working with
- spotlights the layers of limitations

BOUNDARY: *Rivers or streams (water or traffic)*
- creates distinctive flow of movement
- manages the flow of a structure or moment

PRECISENESS: *Walls and fences*
- is the rules or regulations one can go along with, follow, but also fall off, step across and over
- can create invisible or unperceived actors in interactions

IMPROVISATION: *The route (at any given moment)*
- is a contingent, temporary, responsive dialogue
- constantly creates structures in itself that can then be deviated from

SCORE: *the substance of the map*
- is a temporary infrastructure for understanding things
- is a method for recalling structures or responses

Navigation Three:
Emergent Properties of the Moment

The third prompt asks you to begin a walk only using choices of direction determined by your engagement with the intersections of the worded-ideas' elements. For instance, during one moment-ist walk's route, the paving stones (GROWTH) come to the edge of a main road (POWER). Thus, within the meaning-making of the physicality of the moment-ist walk, GROWTH meets POWER. Within the conditions of this third prompt, I choose to use the trajectory of POWER to give direction to my GROWTH. I follow the paving stones around a corner and along the main road until I come to another intersection of worded-ideas and make another choice about the direction. I keep on doing this for thirty minutes. I reflect on the unexpected route my journey created by the logic of the city's streets and my choices: I route around the unfamiliar streets I had never taken before because my walking is usually just the by-product of trying to get somewhere else (to the station, to the bus stop, to the corner shop). The logic of the streets I have just used to inform my choices of direction is thus usually unconsciously present; it is something I absorb about the meaning of where I live but not something I usually recognise or reflect on.

The walks were not intended to provide solutions to ethical conundrums but to find new ways to ask questions about the meaning I made of the city. On one walk, I chose to never engage with the main road (POWER) and just continued to focus on walking on the paving stones (GROWTH). I eventually ended up walking in circles. My reflection was that GROWTH can become a circle or spiral if one does not engage with POWER in a social environment such as London.

There were some incidents when a moment-ist walk left me lost. In those instances, I resisted fitting myself into my pre-existing discourse, movement or pattern and strived to reinterpret the logic of the street, both through the unfamiliarity of my post-Covid body and the unfamiliarity of the location to which the prompts had led me.

I noticed the web of relationships, responses and choices that were starting to overlay my local area, revealing my own meaning-making of the streets. This web became a structure, unique to my individual walking, that was superimposed onto the design of the city. Noticing the material practice of experiencing the city through the walks involved feelings, memories and sensations developed as a result of the interpretation of the lexicon. By assigning the worded-ideas elements of the London streets around me, I was more conscious of my response to the streets. As I walked, I asked myself how I was in the realm of being fully alive, able to creatively respond, to the sensation of the moment of London.

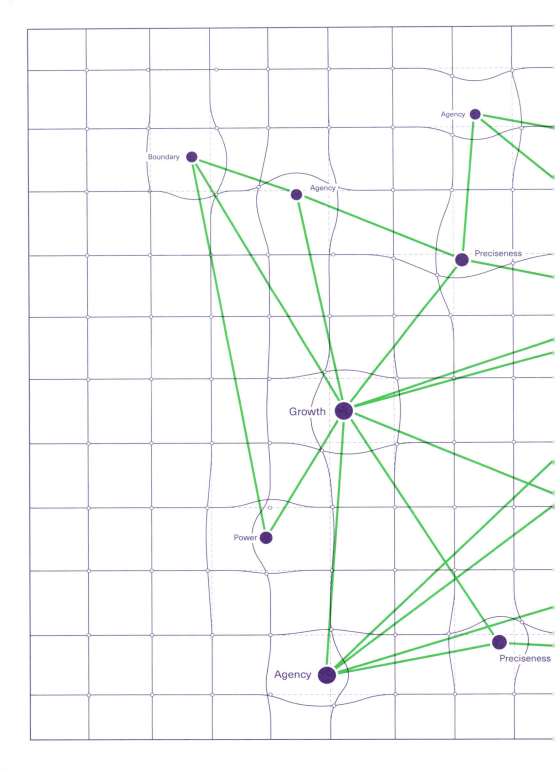

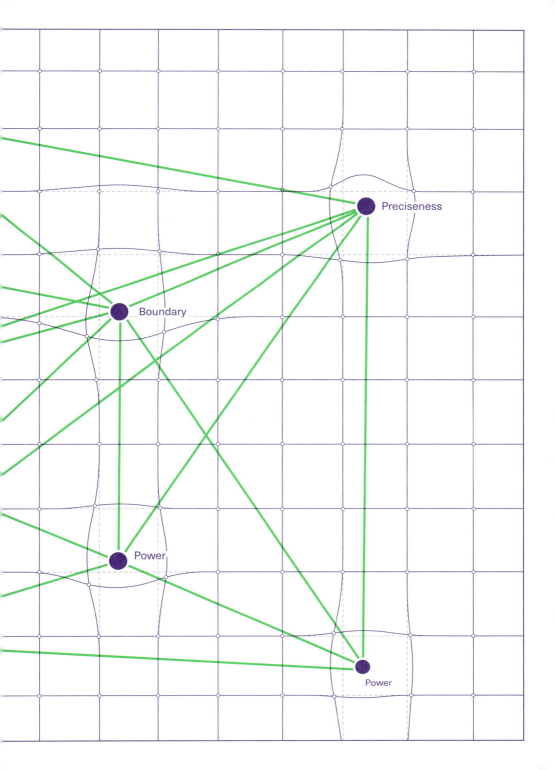

Navigation Three
Map Key

CONNECTEDNESS/SEPARATEDNESS:
The contour intervals on the map
- illustrates the multidimensionality of experience
- exposes the experience of the improvisation of the moment
- lifts experience off the fabric of consciousness into the realm of what is felt: un-camouflages habit, checks instinct and raises response into consciousness, giving it contours and nuance

(AT LEAST) FOUR-DIMENSIONAL DISTANCE:
The grid lines
- contextualises movement (and experience) in the same way the grid lines contextualise a map
- underscores locatable moments of consciousness: moments when dancing makes one more conscious of being in a Place
- locates moments of experience, allowing them to be recallable

AGENCY: *Road junctions*
- influences where one moves from and to, indicates points to begin from or perceived distance from
- is the ability to make choices about the direction/ change of movement and the awareness of the impact of direction and distance on what one perceives to be other than oneself
- involves the direction of movement and the ability to use movement to conjure distance

GROWTH: *Paving stones*
- mosaics into distinguishable structures or ideas
- influences movement in and out of structures and relationships
- generates a sense of accumulation

POWER: *Railway lines and/or main roads*
- has attributes of high velocity and directional movement
- affects points of perception: where one moves from and to
- becomes an invisible or unperceived actor determining connections, actions and relationships

RESISTANCE: *The key to the map*
- shapes understanding of encounter and can be used to confirm presence
- determines the parameters of what one is working with
- spotlights the layers of limitations

BOUNDARY: *Rivers or streams (water or traffic)*
- creates distinctive flow of movement
- manages the flow of a structure or moment
- appears to distort direction because of the flows of movement it temporarily creates

PRECISENESS: *Walls and fences*
- is the rules or regulations one can go along with follow, but also fall off, step across and over
- can create invisible or unperceived actors in interactions
- influences connections across the shape of now

IMPROVISATION: *The route 'at any given moment)*
- is a contingent, temporary, responsive dialogue
- constantly creates structures in itself that can then be deviated from
- belongs to the multifaceted shape of the moment

SCORE: *The substance of the map*
- is a temporary infrastructure for understanding things
- is a method for recalling structures or responses
- is an apparatus for recording or settling a moment

CORRESPONDENCES

04

to note	to exchange
to associate	to communicate

The lexicon I propose in this publication suggests possible starting points for exploring language that sit across the ideas and concerns within a range of disciplines interested in spatial practices. However, the point of my artistic research across the project has not been to find a definitive glossary. The shortfall in communication within the lexicon could be as useful as its successes in capturing a shared notion. The point of the exercise of the lexicon has been to have a communication apparatus that can help excavate shared interests and ideas in spatial practices.

In the previous chapter, ADVENTURES, I shared some of the prompts I used to become more familiar with the worded-ideas of the lexicon. I engaged with the design logic of the city streets to challenge my thinking on how the worded-ideas could interact with each other within the lexicon. Out of this activity, I started to notice the web of experiences I was generating, which left a form of felt narrative on the streets. During my local walks, different moments revealed different logics of design, and I have become increasingly aware of the choices and assumptions I used to make meaning of my presence, history and hopes in the city: I have become more aware of myself in the choreography of the city.

My hope has been to create a trans-disciplinary spatial practice lexicon that can generate unpredictable and unforeseen assemblages of concepts, in the way that the moment-ist walks can generate unexpected links through assemblages of the elements of the city. During the latter part of my Theatrum Mundi fellowship, such an unexpected assemblage has emerged between notions of *moments* and *responsiveness*. In this chapter, I share some of the correspondence between Ellie Cosgrave and me, where we reflect on the notions of moments and responsiveness from our different disciplinary perspectives. This is just one example of the potential of the worded-ideas to generate trans-disciplinary discussion.

During the moment-ist walks, I was surprised that my responses to the everyday encounters with the local streets were governed more by memory (and habit) than by the immediacy of touch, smell or vision. *That is the pavement where I saw the rat*, I thought. *This is the corner where the wall fell down.* The choices I made in those places remained there as memories, and those memories were involved in my subsequent meaning-making at those locations, long after the physical assemblages there had changed. Often my history with the streets located me more than the present moment of the physicality of being in the street. Thus, my memory of sensation, derived from exploration of the lexicon, became a layer of the city, which I started to notice more often than the physical structures themselves.

I found that my practice of the now-ness of dance (dance being in the moment) was paradoxically highlighting memory and anticipation. I was intrigued by the notion of the moment in dance as constant response, and how dance also involved accumulated knowledge (the past) in the fabric of the muscles and bones of the dancer. Dance anticipated the future through the continuity of movements, informing how the dancer engaged with their own weight to keep moving. I wondered where, in the assemblage of the city, there was also this form of a present/past/anticipation responding moment.

Moments and Responsiveness

Dancing the moment in the street: To a slight unevenness of paving cracks and chips, my ankles compensate with the spiral twist of my tendons. I feel the condyles of my upper-leg bones nestling into the meniscus-ed plateaus of my tibia. The chill of cool air stirred by traffic passing by creates a subtle vibration on the skin of the back of my knee. The bow of my back and the lift of my shoulders holding my weight wait for the lights to change. I slide in and out of awareness of us-ness (the moment). All that is here with me is co-composing the multiple AGENCY of the moment.

Moments from engineering: Ellie Cosgrave told me about *bending* moments, and I realised how the word *moment* in engineering differs from my own use of the word. A moment is a measure of bending effect that is instigated when an external force is applied to a structural element. In structural engineering, this is important because it is used to calculate where something should be placed and how much force can be applied.

> *The Moment of a force is a measure of its tendency to cause a body to rotate about a specific point or axis. ...*
>
> *The magnitude of the moment of a force acting about a point or axis is directly proportional to the distance of the force from the point or axis.*[23]

I suggest to Ellie that a dance moment is brought into consciousness through the responsive engineering moment of weight leading to movement.

A 'moment' of weight in dance: At a traffic light at a road junction (AGENCY), on paving stones (GROWTH) at the end of a wall (PRECISENESS), I feel the weight of my body pour into the rotation of a turn that is my artistic response to the traffic held at the red light where the pavement ends. Dancing, I feel the weight of the moment in the heaviness of my breath. Dancing, I am in the momentary axis of the past and future of now. My arm, back, knee, hip, each contributes to the multiples of now-ness that is the moment of turning: a drawing together of the past and the future. And as I catch my weight out of the turn, traffic and I are once more in a forward trajectory.

Ellie and I exchanged letters with reflections on moments.

23 Luebkeman, C.H. and D. Peting (1995, 1996) 'What is a Moment?', *Architectonics: the science of architecture* https://web.mit.edu/4.441/1_lectures/1_lecture5/1 _lecture5.html.

Moment One

London, March 2021

Dear Adesola,

I am sitting with my morning coffee on the balcony attached to my bedroom. Three floors up. I can hear the energetic exchanges of children playing in the school grounds that are just beyond the train line which borders my block of flats. The train line itself is on top of three arches, each enclosed with a brick wall. These bricks form the back wall of a fruit and vegetable distribution centre which supplies London's restaurants. They work under the arches through the night.

At deck level of the arches, just below my eye line, bush-sized weeds creep out from the bricks. Bold and robust. Resolute despite (or perhaps because of) the seeming hostility of their environment. Hardy life for hard places. There had been knotweed before. When I moved in, I was given a certificate to prove it had been eradicated. Threat extinguished, and I have the paperwork to show for it: a legal protection from the living threat that thrives on train lines.

On the far wall of the bridge's deck, there are black and white graffiti tags. Nothing elaborate. Hardy. Weed-like. I sense they are a necessary fixture of the city's railways.

And then a train passes. The main event, an interruption. At eye level, from my vantage point, it obscures the school and the school children. It's a long train, containing a world inside itself: a place in its own right. A place cutting through my place. Welcomed. It is purposeful, fast, clear and direct. A precise moment.

Lots of love,
Ellie Cosgrave

London, March 2021

Dear Ellie,

A moment from my first walk after Covid-19: a precise moment. I went as far as the foot of the hill where the road goes over a railway. I planned to turn there and walk back, but I needed to hover by a low wall at the edge of the road. I sat on its bricks to rest for a moment, then I stood up, placing my hands on the trunk of a tree behind the wall to steady myself. As I stood, I felt a light breeze on my face for the first time in a few weeks. Then, my right leg started to shake. It was a dance of weakness.

The muscles of my upper thigh vibrated in time to some inner rhythm. I stared at my own thigh, and it seemed that its vibration was separate from its action of keeping me standing: as if the leg wasn't quite mine. I realised I was holding my breath as I stared at the vibrating leg. I took an inhale and lifted my eyes to look at the leaves of the tree whose trunk I was holding. My knee twitched as if it was about to fold, then the quivering stopped in my leg and started in the leaves of the tree. I caught a glimpse of myself in the breeze, in the leaves.

This first dance-walk was part of slipping out of illness back into the moment of my body and of reconnecting with the us-ness of the city again. The preciseness of standing there by the wall for a minute revealed to me *myself-in-this-moment*. I registered the beyond of my skin, the outside, which reverberated with great power after weeks of being confined to bed. I felt that I was there.

With trepidation,
Adesola

Moment Two

Dear Adesola

The Train Line in My Garden

It cuts through and over
The places we are in

Passing

    I hear it before
    It is here
    And after
    It has gone

Present

    Tracks we made
    Direct
    Contain
    And create space
    For powerful outsiders

Held

My Train line improvises ...

    Logistics
    And learning
    And playing.

    It is sounds
    Noise
    Art.

It is expression
And vandalism.

    Marking
    Living
    Thriving
    It is eating
    And fighting.

    Through
    Over
    Fleeting
    And resolute.
    [Somewhere]
    Going some[where]
    Interrupting some[where]

Ellie Cosgrave

A Conclusion from an On-Going Journey

Over the period of the fellowship, I have been able to move forward with my practice of dance through addressing it as a spatial practice. This has offered me a sense of relocation, as my ideas have developed choreographically, and a sense of repositioning, as my work has contributed to processes outside of dance.

Across the collaborations that were crucial to this project, dance-movement was a method for noticing time and space. As such, dance-movement was not limited to those trained extensively in the aesthetics of dance (dancers, choreographers) but invited those working in other disciplines of spatial practice (such as architects, urbanists, engineers and curators). It has become clear to me during the research that the city was making with me. The exploration of the lexicon offered me new expressions of movement for sensing myself through response in the ever-emerging moment of Place. This means that we are inescapably responsible for our presence within the emergent moment of Place. The somatic nature of my work with Navigations, and the lexicon created as part of it, has left me feeling that to really experience the emergent properties of the moment, we must understand ourselves as contributing to our belonging to the city and our belonging to the environment, which is possible through our ability to respond. We are not separate from city or environment, not separate from Place: we are a part of it all.

Acknowledgements

The research presented in this publication draws on the programme *Choreographing the City*, initiated by Ellie Cosgrave at the Faculty of Engineering Science at the University College London and subsequently expanded into a collaboration between Ellie and John Bingham-Hall (Director of Theatrum Mundi), establishing a shared project with Theatrum Mundi. I am so thankful to John and Ellie for generously taking my dancer/choreographer perspective seriously and continuing the conversation with me after their research concluded. Their generosity led to me being offered the opportunity to take a section of the larger *Choreographing the City* activity further through the fellowship at Theatrum Mundi. Theatrum Mundi has been an immensely valuable space for discussion, exchange and, importantly, support for transdisciplinary research, to which I am indebted. I am also tremendously grateful to Ellie and John for sharing their thinking on the potential of choreographic methods, processes and perspectives to shape the way movement in cities is understood and designed. The first part of the fellowship, I attempted to speak directly to John and Ellie's provocation of movement in the city that their article presents.

Thank you to Theatrum Mundi – Richard Sennett, Marta Michalowska, John Bingham-Hall, Justinien Tribillon, Elahe Karimnia, Cecily Chua, Andrea Cetrulo, Lou Marcellin, and Marcos Villaba – for all their support, administration, creative thinking and introductions, which provided the imagination and the practical support that enabled me to meet many colleagues across disciplines with shared concerns and hopes for how the city can shape the lives of the beings within it. I reflect on the many conversations and shared dances together from the first part of the fellowship in my monograph *Dance, Architecture, and Engineering: Dance in Dialogue*, published by Bloomsbury in 2021.

Encouraged by Theatrum Mundi, who offered me an extended fellowship, I have gone on to focus on developing the apparatus for noticing how the ideas we were all exploring could find a shared demarcation within our disciplines. This led to asking if it would be useful to look for a lexicon. I began the development of a lexicon during the second part of my fellowship at Theatrum Mundi and my artistic residency at the Arts, Culture, and Technology (ACT) programme at the Massachusetts Institute of Technology (MIT). This residency was supported by a grant from the MIT Center for Arts, Science and Technology (CAST). I would like to take this opportunity to thank John Bingham-Hall and Richard Sennett (Trustee of Theatrum Mundi) for introducing me to Professor Gediminas Urbonas of MIT and opening the possibility for me to take my ideas further at the programme there. I am very thankful to Gediminas for co-writing the grant application and hosting my residency. Thank you also to Katherine Higgins, Marion Cunningham, Marissa Friedman and the teams at ACT and CAST who helped make the first part of my residency at MIT so valuable, despite the ever-changing situation of the Covid-19 pandemic.

I would also like to extend a special thank-you to my conversation partners – Gediminas Urbonas, Ellie Cosgrave, Dianne McIntyre, Richard Sennett, Arianna Mazzeo, Hūfanga 'Ōkusitino Māhina, Scott L. Pratt, John Bingham-Hall and Liz Lerman – who contributed to the series of podcasts *Choreographing the City* at MIT.

I would also like to thank Jayden Ali and Andreas Lang who, during the period of 2020/21, invited me to run a studio at Central Saint Martins College of Art and Design in the Spatial Practice MArch course. Also, thank you to Kate Goodwin, Neba Sere and Akil Scafe-Smith for all our stimulating conversations at this time.

Thank you to Helen Kindred and the artists at DancingStrong Movement Lab – Andrew Hinton, Maga Judd, Ofelia Balogun, Harry Fulleylove, Cheniece Warner, June Ting and Jake Alexander – who helped my ideas flourish, who shared their ideas, who gave their time, energy, bodies and knowledge to further the work, and who have been exploring with me during the past two years of Navigations, particularly during the difficult periods of Covid-19 lockdowns.

All these opportunities augmented the Theatrum Mundi fellowship work, along with the new perspectives of lockdowns, choreographing, rehearsing and performing over the computer screen on Zoom, having long Covid and emerging from my house after months of being in one room. These all gave me a new insight into my responding, present body in the city.

Thank you to Marta Michalowska for her brilliant editing work and her supportive and rigorous belief in this publication and my writing. And thank you to Cecily Chua, Marcos Villalba and Santiago Confalonieri for remaining encouraging and inspiring through all the twists and turns of the writing and design process.

Lastly, thank you to my family, Modupe and Marc, Pat, Kore and Kyi, and particularly my partner, Will, who nursed me through long Covid, supporting me in being able to start to get moving again.

Contributors

ADESOLA AKINLEYE is a dancer, choreographer and artist-scholar. She is Assistant Professor in the School of the Arts, Dance Division, at Texas Woman's University and Visiting Lecturer at the Spatial Practices Department, Central Saint Martins, University of the Arts London. She was Visiting Artist 2020–2022 at the Center for Art, Science, and Technology and Research Affiliate at Art, Culture, and Technology, both at the Massachusetts Institute of Technology. Her career began as a dancer with the Dance Theatre of Harlem Workshop Ensemble, later working with UK companies such as Carol Straker Dance Company and Green Candle Dance Company. She has won awards internationally for her choreographic work. She is Co-Director of DancingStrong Movement Lab. Her recent publications include editing/curating *(re:)claiming ballet* and her monograph *Dance, Architecture, and Engineering: Dance in Dialogue*, published by Bloomsbury in 2021. Adesola was Research Fellow at Theatrum Mundi from 2019 to 2021.

ELLIE COSGRAVE is Director of Research and the Community Interest Company at Publica and Associate Professor of Urban Innovation and Policy at University College London. As an engineer, interdisciplinary researcher, dancer, and trained systems thinker, she is motivated by how scientific endeavour, artistic practice, and policy innovation can combine to create a healthier and fairer society, particularly with respect to gender and just climate transitions.

KATE GOODWIN is a curator, creator, writer, researcher and explorer. She is currently Professor of Practice in Architecture (part-time) at Sydney University. Kate was Head/Curator of Architecture at the Royal Academy of Arts in London until 2021. She is passionate about embodied practices and championing public engagement with architecture and the arts through exhibitions, cross-disciplinary events, commissions, activations and festivals.

HELEN KINDRED is Co-Director of Dancing-Strong Movement Lab and Senior Lecturer at Middlesex University. She is a dance artist-scholar who has been making and performing work internationally over the past twenty-five years. Helen's research examines relationships between somatic practices and improvised performance-making through experiences of body-space-environment.

MARTA MICHALOWSKA is a curator, producer, artist and writer based in London. She has recently completed her debut novel, *Sketching in Ashes*, supported by Arts Council England through the Developing Your Creative Practice programme, and is currently writing her second, *A Tram to the Beach*, both exploring contested territories. Michalowska is Co-Director of Theatrum Mundi and Director of The Wapping Project.

MARCOS VILLALBA is a Spanish graphic designer and photographer. He graduated from Central Saint Martins in 2008 and spent the following decade working in London. He currently resides in Montevideo, Uruguay, where he runs a design studio working with clients across the fields of art, culture, and education, as well as self-initiated projects focused on architecture and urbanism. He collaborates with Theatrum Mundi in digital projects, publications, and exhibitions.

SANTIAGO CONFALONIERI is a Uruguayan creative and graphic designer. He is interested in the different actors that influence contemporary society. He is passionate about collaborative and interdisciplinary projects addressing different aspects of art, culture, and education in order to generate different discourses and alternative ways of inhabiting society. He currently works at Villalba Studio and is studying Visual Communication Design at the Universidad de la República in Uruguay.

Editor: Marta Michalowska
Design: Marcos Villalba and Santiago Confalonieri
Proofreading: Imogen Free and Sriwhana Spong
Typeface: Neue Haas Unica
Printing: Print Love ltd

This work is subject to copyright. All rights reserved. No part of this publication may be reproduced, translated, stored in a retrieval system, or transmitted in any form or by any means, electronic or mechanical, without prior written permission from Theatrum Mundi.

Copyright © Adesola Akinleye, 2022

The right of Adesola Akinleye to be identified as the author of this work has been asserted in accordance with Section 77 of the Copyright, Design and Patents Act 1988.

ISBN: 978-1-3999-4019-1

This publication is part of Theatrum Mundi Editions, a series reflecting current streams and new directions in our research, led by our team and collaborators, and shared with our members. Editions are generously supported by the Friends of Theatrum Mundi.

Friends of Theatrum Mundi
(see https://theatrum-mundi.org/become-a-member/)

MA Cities, Central Saint Martins
Rudi Christian Ferreira
Catherine Visser
David Chipperfield Architects
Joao Villas

With special thanks to our patron Nick Tyler

Theatrum Mundi
c/o Groupwork
15A Clerkenwell Close
EC1R 0AA
London, UK

Theatrum Mundi Europe
59 Rue du Département
75018
Paris, France